DK READERS

Level 2

Level 3

A Note to Parents

DK READERS is a compelling program for beginning readers, designed in conjunction with leading literacy experts, including Dr. Linda Gambrell, Distinguished Professor of Education at Clemson University. Dr. Gambrell has served as President of the National Reading Conference, the College Reading Association, and the International Reading Association.

Beautiful illustrations and superb full-color photographs combine with engaging, easy-to-read stories to offer a fresh approach to each subject in the series. Each DK READER is guaranteed to capture a child's interest while developing his or her reading skills, general knowledge, and love of reading.

The five levels of DK READERS are aimed at different reading abilities, enabling you to choose the books that are exactly right for your child:

Pre-level 1: Learning to read
Level 1: Beginning to read
Level 2: Beginning to read alone
Level 3: Reading alone
Level 4: Proficient readers

The "normal" age at which a child begins to read can be anywhere from three to eight years old. Adult participation through the lower levels is very helpful for providing encouragement, discussing storylines, and sounding out unfamiliar words.

No matter which level you select, you can be sure that you are helping your child learn to read, then read to learn!

DK

LONDON, NEW YORK, MUNICH,
MELBOURNE, AND DELHI

Editor Catherine Saunders
Designer Lisa Robb
Pre-Production Producer Marc Staples
Producer Louise Daly
Design Manager Nathan Martin
Publishing Manager Julie Ferris
Art Director Ron Stobbart
Publishing Director Simon Beecroft

Reading Consultant
Linda B. Gambrell, PH.D.

First American Edition, 2013
13 14 15 16 17 10 9 8 7 6 5 4 3 2 1
Published in the United States by DK Publishing
375 Hudson Street, New York, New York 10014

LEGO and the LEGO logo are trademarks of the LEGO Group
© 2013 The LEGO Group
Produced by Dorling Kindersley under license
from the LEGO Group.

001–187430–Aug/13

DK books are available at special discounts when purchased in bulk
for sales promotions, premiums, fund-raising, or educational use.
For details, contact:
DK Publishing Special Markets
375 Hudson Street
New York, New York 10014
SpecialSales@dk.com

A catalog record for this book is available
from the Library of Congress.

ISBN: 978-1-4654-0265-3 (Paperback)
ISBN: 978-1-4654-0266-0 (Hardcover)

Printed and bound in China by L. Rex

Discover more at
www.dk.com
www.LEGO.com

Contents

DK READERS

LEGO HERO FACTORY

Brain Attack

Written by Catherine Saunders

Hero Factory

The Hero Factory is one of the busiest places in Makuhero City. New robots are built here every day. They learn how to use many different weapons, ride speed cycles, and fly special spacecraft known as Hero Pods. The training is tough, and only the best robots become heroes.

Hero Core

A robot hero comes to life when a special rock is placed inside its body. The rock is known as Quaza.

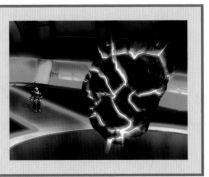

A robot hero's job is to keep people safe. However, in a far corner of the galaxy an evil plan is forming. Soon, the heroes will face a dangerous mission.

Uh oh! Someone has stolen the plans for the Hero Factory.

Plasma blade

Rocka is one of the newest members of the team. He is brave, but impulsive.

Hero Core

Alpha 1 Team

The smartest and toughest robot heroes become members of Alpha 1 Team. These heroes are the best in the galaxy. The team has been on lots of exciting missions and saved the galaxy many times.

Preston Stormer is the leader of Alpha 1 Team. He is a famous hero. He plans missions and tells the other heroes what to do.

Shoulder missiles

Ice blade

Ice weapon

Stormer

The newest heroes in Alpha 1 Team are known as rookies. They are brave, tough robots, but they have been on fewer missions than the other heroes.

Furno XL is a rookie, but he has already won an underwater battle with Jawblade.

Fire sword

Fire shield

Furno XL

Bow staff

Spinning
blade shield

Breez

Breez is a
rookie and
the only female
member of Alpha 1
Team. She is skilled
in communication and
negotiation, as well as combat.

Each robot hero has been programmed with a unique skill. Rookie Evo can communicate with almost any computer or machine. That means he can disarm many foes without needing to fight.

Pincer weapon

Small dagger

Evo

Bulk

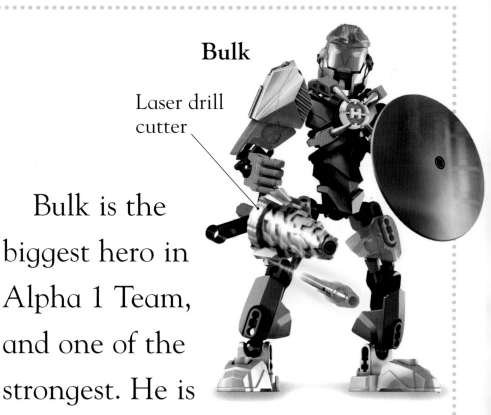

Laser drill
cutter

Bulk is the biggest hero in Alpha 1 Team, and one of the strongest. He is a brave and experienced hero. Bulk likes to be at the center of the action.

Young rookie
Surge is also a rookie. He wields an electricity shooter. Highly charged Surge often gets a little bored between missions!

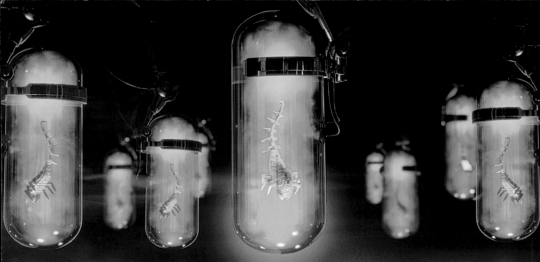

Somewhere in the galaxy, in a secret lab, something evil is growing. It looks like brains!

New mission

When Alpha 1 Team isn't on missions, the team goes out to meet the ordinary citizens of Makuhero City. Most heroes like talking to the public, but Surge would rather be out fighting villains. The rookie robot is about to get his wish!

While the heroes are busy meeting the public, the mysterious Brains are on the move. They leave the lab via small space pods and blast off in all directions. The brave heroes of Alpha 1 Team have no idea what is happening, but they will find out soon enough...

First victim

This peaceful ogre is happily passing his time in a smelly swamp when an alien pod lands nearby. As Ogrum cautiously sniffs the strange craft, a Brain leaps out and attaches itself to his head!

The ogre tries to fight the Brain, but it is too strong. Soon the Brain is in control of Ogrum. It has the power to make him do whatever it wants.

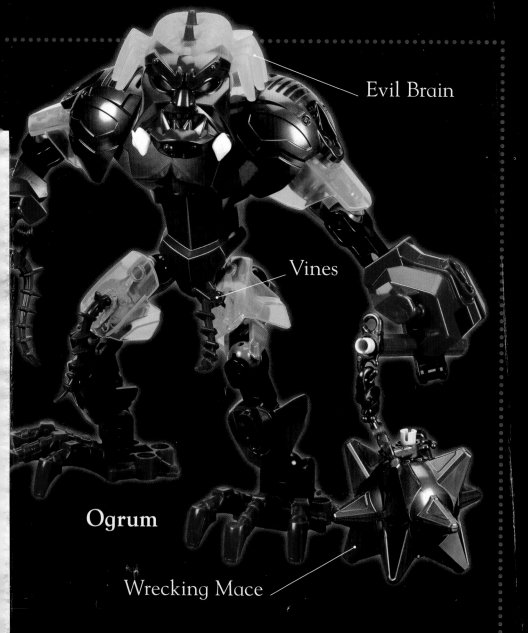

Evil Brain

Vines

Ogrum

Wrecking Mace

The Brain's true plans are not
yet known, but one thing is
certain—it's definitely evil!

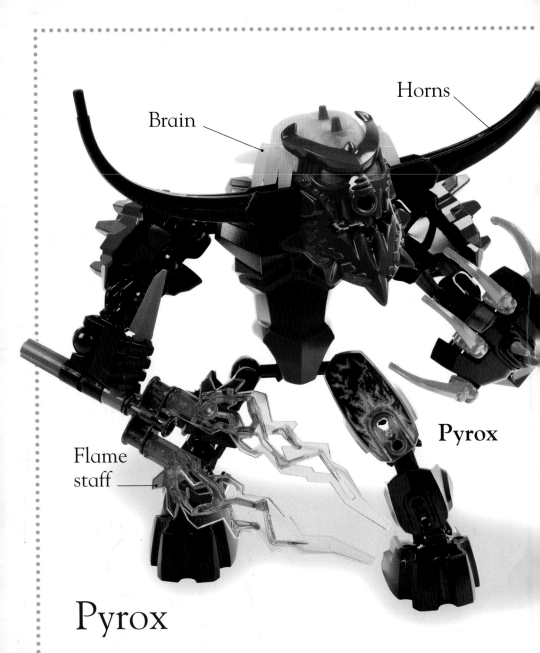

Brain

Horns

Flame
staff

Pyrox

Pyrox

In a volcanic part of the galaxy, an evil Brain discovers a powerful horned fire beast.

Pyrox can shoot flames from his arm cannons, but he is actually a very gentle beast.

The Brain can't wait to use Pyrox's powers for its own evil purposes. It attaches itself to the fire beast and takes control of him.

Evil signs

There are several clues that a creature is under the control of an evil Brain. Not only will there be a Brain attached to its head, but its eyes will also glow red.

Desert attack

Scarox lives in the hot desert sand. He moves like a spider, and the razor sharp spikes at the end of his arms can pierce solid rock.

Few creatures can survive in the desert, but Scarox is tough. However, when he goes to an oasis in search of water, he doesn't expect to be attacked by a Brain! Even the mighty Scarox can't withstand the power of an evil Brain.

The Brain hopes that Scarox's
sharp spikes will be able to
pierce armor as easily as rocks!

Brain

Sharp
spike

Scarox

Ice to see you

One Brain travels to the coldest part of the galaxy to find its unlucky victim.

Brain

Ice shovel

Ice claw

Frost Beast

Frost Beast is one of the few
creatures who can survive in the
freezing region. He carries an ice
shovel which he uses to clear
snow and ice from his path.
It can also be used as a weapon,
along with his ice claws.

However, what really attracts
the evil Brain to Frost Beast is
the creature's freezing breath.
It could be a very useful weapon,
so the Brain attaches itself to
Frost Beast. Brrrrr! Even evil
Brains feel the cold!

Rock giant

Bruizer looks like a fierce giant, but he is a very sensitive and creative creature. He is so strong that he can crush rocks, but he actually prefers to make interesting sculptures with them. However, when an evil Brain sees the mighty Bruizer, it's not his art skills that attract it.

The Brain attacks Bruizer and takes control of him. Now Bruizer prefers smashing rocks to sculpting them!

Bruizer

Powerful fists

Brain

Rock
armor

Ocean prey

Even ocean creatures aren't safe from the Brains. Aquagon is a shy sea creature who spends most of his days hiding behind a coral reef. He is so timid that he is even frightened of fish!

However, one Brain sees evil potential in Aquagon. It attaches itself to the harmless sea creature and turns him from meek to monster. Aquagon is no longer scared of fish—in fact he's not scared of anything at all.

The Brain has a mission for Aquagon: He must head for dry land—to Makuhero City!

Brain

Sea blade

Aquagon

Powerful host

One lucky Brain finds a huge and extremely powerful host lurking in a dark cave.

Brain

Dragon
Bolt

The cave is home to Dragon Bolt, and even this mighty beast cannot resist the evil Brain. The Brain soon takes control of the dragon. Now they can join the other Brains.

Wings

Finally, their evil purpose is clear. The Brains and their host creatures are all heading toward Makuhero City. In fact, they are heading to the Hero Factory and have the stolen plans!

Brain attack!

All over the galaxy, thousands of poor, innocent creatures are under the control of the evil Brains. Unfortunately, they are all heading to the Hero Factory! It's time for the heroes to fight.

The Brains and their creatures are leaving a trail of damage and destruction.

At first the heroes are puzzled: Why would these normally friendly creatures attack them? Then Rocka notices the Brains and the red eyes. Alpha 1 Team has a difficult mission ahead.

Mission control

Zib and Quadal support the heroes. They upgrade their weapons to help them battle the Brains.

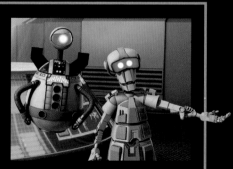

The heroes have a problem—
how can they defeat the Brains
without hurting the creatures?
Bulk finds the solution. When
he hits the second red spike on
the Brain, it lets go!

Bulk tells the other heroes
what he has learned, but it's not
easy to get close to the Brains.

Rocka has a new jet pack.
It's perfect for taking
down Dragon Bolt.

Eventually the heroes succeed
in their mission. They remove
all the Brains, and the creatures
return home. The Hero Factory
is safe again, for now.

Quiz

1. What has been stolen from the Hero Factory?

2. Who is the only female member of Alpha 1 Team?

3. Which poor rock giant is attacked by a Brain?

4. Which of the Brain's victims is a shy sea creature?

5. Which robot hero has a jet pack?

1. The plans for the factory 2. Breez 3. Bruizer 4. Aquagon 5. Rocka

Index